AROUND
WITNEY
IN OLD PHOTOGRAPHS

PREPARE YOURSELF FOR A TRIP AROUND OLD WITNEY, when motor cars vied with horse-drawn carts for the road – in the days long before the new bypass. This Ford van and its driver were photographed by Witney photographer, George Pickett.

AROUND
WITNEY
IN OLD PHOTOGRAPHS

COLLECTED BY
CHRIS MITCHELL

ALAN SUTTON

Alan Sutton Publishing Limited
Phoenix Mill · Far Thrupp · Stroud · Gloucestershire

First Published 1990

British Library Cataloguing in Publication Data

Around Witney in old photographs.
1. Oxfordshire. Witney region, history
I. Mitchell, Chris
942.571

ISBN 0-86299-811-5

Typeset in 9/10 Korinna.
Typesetting and origination by
Alan Sutton Publishing Limited.
Printed in Great Britain by
Dotesios Printers Limited.

CONTENTS

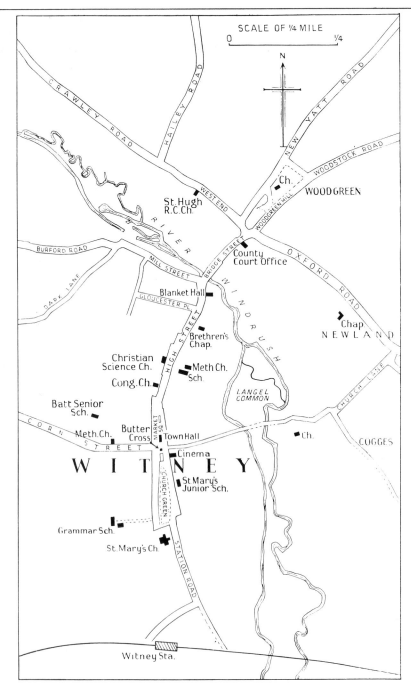

SCALE OF ¼ MILE

OUTLINE STREET PLAN of Witney.

INTRODUCTION

I have heard Witney described as a 'sleepy little market town nestling in the Cotswolds'. Yet in its heyday the town was served by the Great Western Railway, supported two breweries and, more recently, even boasted its own aerodrome which was a vital repair base during the Second World War. Also for more than five hundred years Witney has been, and still is, home to a major manufacturing industry: the words 'Witney' and 'blankets' frequently go hand in hand. So although it may be true that Witney has a peaceful rural atmosphere, I hope this book will show that the town has been anything but sleepy. Today it is still the combination of traditional market town and modern thriving commercial centre that gives Witney its unique charm. However, I have not concentrated on Witney alone but have taken in all those surrounding villages that look to Witney as their local town – north as far as Ramsden, east to Combe, south to Bampton, and west to Asthall.

All the photographs in this book have been drawn from my collection of over two thousand picture postcards of the Witney area which has been amassed over the last eighteen years. Most of us send postcards when we go on holiday, but in the 1900s both the sending and receiving of postcards was a national craze. A postcard album was a common feature in most homes. This is why many postcards from the Edwardian era simply bear the message 'Another one for your album'. Others, though, describe graphically the events they depict: events often of great significance at the time but which have since been long forgotten. Wherever possible I have included these messages along with the photographs.

The value of the photographs used for picture postcards cannot be under-estimated. From the turn of the century until the 1920s millions were produced every year. They were both cheap and convenient. With a halfpenny stamp and several postal collections and deliveries daily they provided not only a means by which news could be conveyed rapidly, but also a vivid record of local landscapes and events.

I have laid this book out as if it were a leisurely stroll around the town. Some readers may enjoy retracing my steps and seeing for themselves those places where time has stood still and those where its passing has left its mark. The visits to surrounding villages may perhaps be seen as cycle tours – another popular pastime of the era. There are also sections on the woollen industry; special events, including the Mop Fair; and 'Oddments' which includes a few of my favourite pictures of bygone life in Witney.

I hope these photographs will revive memories for some and bring familiar places to life for others, as they have done for me.

Witney: the Northern End

WITNEY VIEWED FROM THE OXFORD ROAD. The telegraph poles, carts and trees have long since disappeared.

THE RIVER WINDRUSH from Cogges, before it enters the town.

ANOTHER VIEW OF THE RIVER showing the footbridge that separates Cogges from Witney. To the left you can just make out Cogges church and other buildings.

Cogges & Windrush.

A CLOSER VIEW OF COGGES CHURCH, the Priory and St Mary House (beyond the Manor Farm, now Cogges Farm Museum).

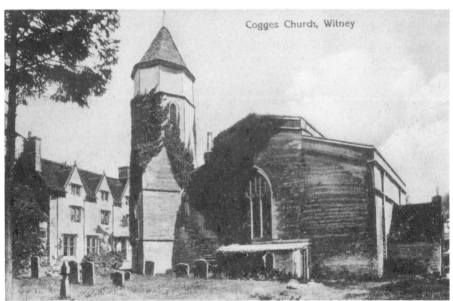

Cogges Church, Witney

THE EARLY ENGLISH STYLE CHURCH AT COGGES. The building alongside is known as the Priory and parts of it date back to the twelfth century. The incumbent in 1915 was the Revd R. Hodgell.

NEWLAND IN THE PARISH OF ST MARY COGGES consists of one long street diverging from Bridge Street and extending to the top of Oxford Hill.

Newland, Witney. 908.

NEWLAND VIEWED FROM OUTSIDE THE PIKE HOUSE on the corner of Church Lane. The house was pulled down in the 1947 road-widening scheme.

NEWLAND BEFORE THE ROAD WAS WIDENED in 1947. Messrs Fifield and Son, motor car proprietors, ran their business from the garage at the top of the road on the left. They offered 'Austin Motor Hearses and Limousines for hire'.

THE JUNCTION OF WOODGREEN HILL (sometimes known as Broad Hill), West End and Bridge Street. The building on the extreme left, now called Staple Hall, was originally a coaching inn.

THE OLD HOUSE ON THE HILL, C. 1900.

WOODGREEN AT THE TOP OF BROAD HILL. The green is divided by the New Yatt Road. On the left are the caravans and tent of the Welsh Revival Movement.

THE SMALL GREEN showing Holy Trinity church, which was built in 1849, partly by public subscription. It seats 518 persons.

TRINITY COTTAGE, NARROW HILL, on the immediate right. On the far left is the Three Pigeons public house, and on the right the recreation ground.

Trinity Church Wood Green, Witney

HOLY TRINITY CHURCH, this time from the recreation ground. Three people pose artistically for the photographer.

SOME OF THE FINER GEORGIAN TOWN HOUSES OF WITNEY. On the far left of both pictures is The Gables which now houses the West Oxfordshire District Council offices.

WOODSTOCK ROAD, c. 1910.

WOODSTOCK ROAD, c. 1915.

WEST END LOOKING TOWARDS CRAWLEY. Children could certainly not play with their dog in the street today!

THE FAR END OF WEST END. The prominent building on the right was a toll-house. The road continues on to Crawley or, if you bear right, to the village of Hailey.

WEST END HAS NOT CHANGED THAT MUCH, although it would have been unusual to have found it free of traffic even in 1912.

AN EARLY POSTCARD VIEW OF WEST END. It was sent by someone called Alice and reads 'The view is West Street, the house on the right hand corner is where I used to go to music'.

AN EARLY VIEW OF BRIDGE STREET from the bridge, showing a group of men outside Middleton's Gentlemen's Outfitters, No. 24 Bridge Street. Later the shop passed into the hands of Cook and Boggis, cash drapers; it is now part of the Court Inn.

ANOTHER VIEW OF THE STREET, but this time nearer to the bridge. The shop on the left is a newsagents. The billboard outside reads 'Daily Mail. Five £250 cheques – Do the Govt fully realise?'

THIS VIEW OF BRIDGE STREET shows Walker's newsagents, No. 15 Bridge Street, who were the publishers of the photograph. A billboard reads 'Cabinet split over Egypt'.

BRIDGE STREET LOOKING FROM WEST END and Narrow Hill towards the bridge. On the left is the county court (No. 28) and beyond that the Black Head Inn. To the right is Smith's grocery.

A VIEW OF BRIDGE STREET before the bridge was altered. The houses on the immediate right were demolished to make way for Smith's Bridge Street Mill.

A VIEW OF SMITH'S BRIDGE STREET MILL.

THE ORIGINAL BRIDGE viewed from the Windrush. The waters of the River Windrush are said to possess special qualities which contributed to the whiteness and softness of the blankets manufactured in the area.

Witney Bridge – View from front door of Riverside.

THE BRIDGE FROM THE OTHER SIDE, viewed from the front door of Riverside, the house which can be seen behind the bridge in the picture above.

The Bridge, Witney.

THE BRIDGE BEFORE IT WAS ALTERED, looking down Bridge Street towards West End. Not only was it widened but the 'hump' was also significantly reduced. On the left are the premises of James Marriott, coal, coke, anthracite and salt factors.

Witney, New Bridge.

NEW BRIDGE, complete with ornamental lighting and railings. It was altered again in later years.

ANOTHER VIEW OF NEW BRIDGE, this time from Mill Street. The sign reads 'Caution. Road repairs in progress. Drive slowly.'

MILL STREET LOOKING EAST. Note the gas lighting and, in the distance, the chimney of Messrs Charles Early's mill, which can still be seen today. The house railings disappeared to aid the war effort during the Second World War.

AN AERIAL PHOTOGRAPH OF CHARLES EARLY'S MILLS. Note the extent of the works and also the blankets drying on the frames.

AN EARLIER VIEW OF WITNEY MILLS from Dark Lane.

THE WATER TOWER AT THE TOP OF TOWER HILL. The view is a postcard and reads 'Just fancy the Water Tower has burst again, the union [workhouse] was flooded and the house next to it as well.' The water tower obviously had its problems. It was opened in 1903, burst in 1904, and again shortly afterwards.

The Aerodrome, Witney.

THE AERODROME ON BURFORD ROAD was used in both the First and Second World Wars. The site is now occupied by the Smiths factory and the industrial estate. The aircraft pictured are de Havillands – the firm had a factory on the aerodrome in the 1940s.

The High Street and the Market Place

E.A. LONG'S MOTOR AND CYCLE WORKS, adjacent to the bridge. They hired out trailers and cycles and also acted as undertakers and wheelwrights.

THE WESTERN END OF HIGH STREET, showing the bridge and Blanket Hall. It is hardly changed today.

ANOTHER VIEW OF THE WESTERN END OF HIGH STREET. The public house on the immediate right is the Plough, which was owned by Clinch & Co. The beer was brewed locally at the Eagle Brewery, Market Square. Beyond is the Kings Arms public house.

THE BLANKET HALL, HIGH STREET. The building dates from 1710 and was erected to weigh, measure and market the blankets manufactured in the area. Note the one-handed clock.

A PHOTOGRAPH OF CHARLES WIGGINS'S SHOP in the High Street. He was a china and glass dealer as well as a fellmonger, selling dressed animal skins and hides.

AN EARLY PHOTOGRAPH OF MID-HIGH STREET. At this time it was mainly residential, with the shops coming later.

A VIEW OF THE HIGH STREET. On the left is Henry Long and Sons' ironmongery. Long had shops at Nos 69 and 85 High Street.

THE HIGH STREET, with the Methodist church on the immediate right.

HIGH STREET AND THE METHODIST CHURCH (note the mature trees). The photograph is a postcard, and reads 'Just another one of dear old Witney, the place where I learnt all my wickedness.'

THE METHODIST CHURCH AND SCHOOL. This is to undergo major alteration and change of use in the near future and will provide further commercial premises for the town.

THE SOUTHERN END OF HIGH STREET, c. 1929.

AN EARLY VIEW OF THE HIGH STREET IN FLOOD. The building on the left with iron railings in front, which is partially obscured, was the old Congregational chapel. This was pulled down in 1971 and a supermarket built in its place.

THE HIGH STREET IN FLOOD, July 1915. The floods were caused by poor drainage, rather than by rain. The building on the far right is Knights Machine and Printing Works. Next door is the Witney Gas Company building.

MORE FLOODS IN THE HIGH STREET. The building on the immediate right is J. Brice & Son, sanitary plumber. Outside someone is attending to the drains.

UPPER HIGH STREET LOOKING TOWARDS THE HILL, 26 June 1905. The floods did not seem to deter haymaking or the use of the road.

THE HIGH STREET FROM THE HILL. Boots the chemist remains on the same site today, although the ownership of many of the other shops has changed.

A HORSE AND CART OUTSIDE MEADOWSWEET STORES (owned by Goodwin Foster and Co. Ltd), grocers, No. 34 High Street. Next door is Alfred Usher's shop (proprietor J.J. Burford), stationer and bookseller, No. 32 High Street.

THE HIGH STREET, c. 1900. At that time the Central Café was still the Temperance Hotel. Cook and Boggis's tailors shop was replaced by Waitrose's supermarket in the mid-1960s.

THE HIGH STREET, c. 1920. On the immediate right is the Cross Keys Hotel (landlord S.C. Fisher). Beyond is the Central Café and Commercial Hotel.

THE HILL, FROM OPPOSITE MARKET SQUARE. On the right is Chas. Jackson's shop, No. 48 Market Square. He was a confectioner.

LOOKING DOWN THE HILL FROM BATT HOUSE. On the left is the doctor's house (now the new post office) and beyond this the old post office (now Denton's shop).

A FINAL VIEW OF THE HIGH STREET, most likely in the late 1930s. The building on the immediate left is the old post office, opposite the Boots building. Boots' sign advertises 'insurance dispensing' (i.e. of prescriptions under the National Insurance Scheme).

F.O. WHITCHER'S SHOP, which disappeared to make way for the National Westminster Bank. In 1963 three houses next to the shop were demolished during the construction of Welch Way. Mr Whitcher carried on trading for a while after this, until eventually his shop and Harris's fish shop next door were modernized to form the present bank.

THIS PHOTOGRAPH is believed to be of the Wesleyan School treat. The shop centre left is Walker's grocery, No. 5 High Street.

A MARCH IN THE HIGH STREET. The trade union banner suggests they may have been workers on strike.

HORSE-DRAWN TRANSPORT IN THE HIGH STREET, September 1905.

HIGH STREET VIEWED FROM THE HILL, C. 1930.

ON THE IMMEDIATE LEFT IS THE COMMERCIAL HOTEL (formerly the Temperance Hotel and the Central Café). Next door is the Cross Keys public house.

COOK AND BOGGIS'S SHOP, c. 1905. This was one of the more important shops in the town.

THE HILL, WITNEY, c. 1940.

THE MARKET SQUARE FROM OUTSIDE THE MARLBOROUGH HOTEL. The shop on the far right is Neave and Lea, chemist, druggist and optician, No. 49 Market Square.

AN EARLIER VIEW OF THE MARKET SQUARE. The square is open to the High Street and gas lamps are in evidence.

THIS EARLY PHOTOGRAPH OF CHILDREN in the Market Square was produced by J.T. Bridgeman, portrait and landscape photographer.

A HORSE AND CART OUTSIDE THE BANK on the Hill opposite the Market Square. The view is a postcard and reads 'Will this do for your collection?'

THE CORONATION PROCESSION GOING UP BATT HILL in June 1911. There were at least 1,600 people taking part in the procession.

ANOTHER PROCESSION, this time in 1906. The photograph is a postcard and the sender was obviously anxious that he should be identified, having marked the picture and given clear instructions on the reverse as to how he could be located.

A FORTNIGHTLY MARKET for cattle, sheep and pigs was held in the Market Square and a corn market was held there weekly on Thursdays. Both were well attended.

Witney Market

July 20 04

WITNEY MARKET in 1904. In the centre is Valentine and Barrell's, tailors. Mr Valentine also owned another shop in the square.

WITNEY MARKET one year later.

THE MARKET. On the extreme right is Moore's shop, organ and piano repairers, then Hiltons, boot and shoe suppliers, and beyond that again the Market Restaurant.

THE MARKET SQUARE IN THE LATE 1940s. The square is still open to the High Street, but the cattle market is severely depleted.

ANOTHER VIEW OF THE MARKET SQUARE. In the centre you can see W.T. Ransom's, the chemists, Currys' radio and cycle shop and the Cadel Library. The Cadel premises are now occupied by the Anglia Building Society.

THE HILL. On the immediate left next to Tarrant's grocery is the Marlborough Arms Hotel, which was run by Lewis Percival Collett. Beyond is Whitehead's, the jewellers, with its blinds drawn.

A HENRY TAUNT PHOTOGRAPH of the Market Square, the Hill and the High Street. Of special interest is Neave's shop on the far right. His partner has changed once again; this time it is Davy.

THE MARKET SQUARE in the 1920s. The building at the back of the square next to the Corn Exchange is Rowley's, house furnisher, cabinet maker and undertaker (Nos 21–9 Market Square). This shop was later pulled down and modernized (see opposite), and is now the Co-op.

THE MARKET SQUARE in 1933. The building in the centre was occupied by the City of Oxford Motor Services Ltd in association with the Great Western Railway Co. Above was Burton's hairdresser and tobacconist. At this time cars were not allowed to park in the square.

FIFTEEN YEARS LATER and the square is little changed.

THE MARKET SQUARE LOOKING TOWARDS THE CHURCH. Immediately behind the Buttercross are the tea rooms and the shop of T.E. Wickham, draper and tailor.

WITNEY CARNIVAL in 1933, with people waiting by the Buttercross for the procession to pass. In the background is the Pearl Assurance Co. building (No. 25 Market Square).

The Buttercross and Church Green

A GROUP OF CHILDREN posing for the photographer at the Buttercross. In the background is Valentine & Barrell's shop.

THE BUTTERCROSS AND TOWN HALL. The Town Hall was repaired in 1876. It is a small rectangular building in stone, consisting of one large chamber supported on nine columns, the lower stage forming an open piazza.

LEIGH & SON'S IRONMONGERY SHOP was owned and operated by the Leigh family for five generations. It remained unchanged until 1978, when Ian Leigh had the shop modernized.

CORN STREET FROM THE BUTTERCROSS. On the left Leigh's shop – on the opposite corner Tarrant's shop. The Tarrants were grocers and had traded in Witney since before 1869.

THE BUTTERCROSS. Blankets being transported by horse-drawn carts.

A PASSENGER COACH passing between the Buttercross and the Town Hall.

HORSE-DRAWN CART belonging to W.H. Tarrant & Sons, wholesale grocer, off-loading goods at their shop opposite the Town Hall.

Market Square and Town Hall, Witney

PASSENGER COACH standing outside Tarrant's shop. Passengers alighted here for the Marlborough (Marlboro) Hotel. The photograph is a postcard and reads 'I went this afternoon to see the Boys Brigade reviewed by General French in the Park.'

Butter Cross, Town Hall, Market Square, Witney.

THE BUTTERCROSS viewed from the Witney Blanket Co. premises, No. 39 Market Square (now Lloyds Bank). The company moved from here to the Leys premises in 1921.

THE TOWN HALL and, to the left, Dingle & Sons, boot and shoe retailer, No. 51 Market Square. The shop remained on these premises until very recently.

THE CORN EXCHANGE and adjoining shops before it was abandoned. It lost its railing during the Second World War and the balcony is no longer in place on the restored building.

THE CORN EXCHANGE IN MARKET SQUARE was erected in 1863 by a public company, at a cost of £2,500. On the ground floor is a market hall, with offices and retiring rooms, where assemblies, balls, exhibitions and public meetings were held.

THE BUTTERCROSS in the 1920s. To the right you can see the Electric Theatre and to the left is the Habgoods building which was later demolished to provide access to the Waitrose supermarket and other buildings.

THE ELECTRIC THEATRE, latterly known as the Palace, prior to its opening in the 1920s. In the 1930s the times of opening were 5.45 p.m. until 10.15 p.m., and prices of admission to the stalls were 6d., 1s., 1s. 3d. and to the balcony 1s. 6d. and 1s. 10d. It finally closed in 1985.

THE BUTTERCROSS — looking down the west side of Church Green with St Mary's church in the background.

THE WAR MEMORIAL, dedicated in 1919, commemorates Witney people who died in the First World War.

THE WAR MEMORIAL, THE BULL INN AND THE ANGEL PUBLIC HOUSE. Note the splendid array of vehicles. Behind the bus you can just see Saltmarsh and Druce's shop (No. 44 Church Green). They were grocers, wine and spirit merchants, tobacconists and patent medicine vendors.

THE WAR MEMORIAL from Church Green. In the centre you can see a Lyons Tea van on the car park where vehicles continue to park to the present day.

THE WAR MEMORIAL – looking down towards the hill. Beyond is the High Street.

THE EAST SIDE OF CHURCH GREEN showing the Fleece Hotel. In 1939 the hotel was run by William George Esling.

CHURCH GREEN in the early 1950s. Beyond the lady coming out of the Fleece Hotel is a vehicle belonging to the Swan Laundry, which was in Corn Street.

THE FLEECE HOTEL, No. 11 Church Green. It was previously known as the Fleece Commercial Hotel.

CHURCH GREEN in the early 1930s.

ST MARY'S CHURCH AND ALMSHOUSES. The tower contains eight bells dating from 1660 to 1815 and a clock, bought by public subscription in 1876, at a cost of £195.

ST MARY'S CHURCH VIEWED ACROSS CHURCH GREEN, c. 1919. The delivery cycle belongs to Swingburn Ltd, baker and confectioner, No. 9 Market Square.

CHILDREN AT PLAY ON CHURCH GREEN, June 1903.

SHEEP GRAZING ON CHURCH GREEN, November 1905.

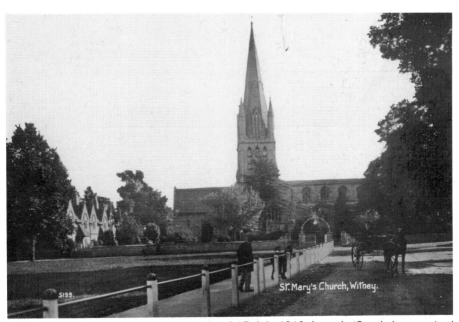

A VIEW OF THE CHURCH FROM A POSTCARD dated 17 July 1910. It reads 'So glad you arrived home before lighting up time and escaped the bobby.' It continues 'Mother and I cycled to Swindon, Tuesday afternoon, about fifty miles in all so we consider we have done well.'

AERIAL PHOTOGRAPH OF WITNEY CHURCH looking north, taken in the 1920s. The picture was produced by a company based in Hendon, Middlesex.

BIRD'S-EYE VIEW OF THE PARISH CHURCH. The Early English tower with its massive turret pinnacles and tall, elegant windows, the lofty clerestories and the transepts, set among the trees, make for a classic picture.

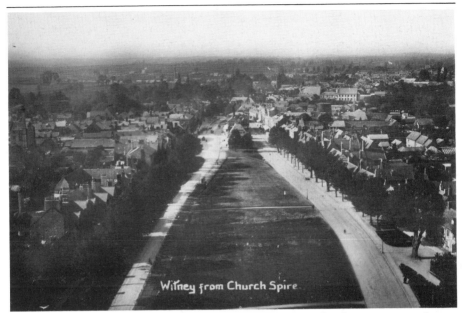

WITNEY VIEWED FROM THE CHURCH TOWER, c. 1912. It you look closely you can see the gas holder in Gas Lane (centre right).

'WITNEY IN WINTER'. This photograph was produced as a postcard by the Cadel Library in January 1918. The card reads 'This was the deepest snow we have had all at once for many years. It was over a foot deep, it came on the Tuesday night, 15th January 1918, when Ern went back to France. Next day we could scarce get to work being near knee deep.'

THE POLICE STATION, on the west side of Church Green, was erected in 1860, at a cost of £2,500. It had a large room, in which petty sessions were held. The station also included houses for the inspector and a sergeant, guard-rooms and cells.

THE GRAMMAR SCHOOL, founded in 1663 by Henry Box, citizen and grocer of London and native of Witney.

THE GRAMMAR SCHOOL, winter 1924. Regrettably most of these trees have now disappeared.

THE GRAMMAR SCHOOL AGAIN. Originally it took just thirty boys from the parish, and was reconstituted in 1877 as a co-educational secondary school until it was taken over by the County Council in 1939.

THE WEST SIDE OF CHURCH GREEN.

THE RURAL DISTRICT COUNCIL OFFICES on Church Green (1939). At this time Major Guy Feildon from Cokethorpe Park, Ducklington, was chairman of the council.

THE UNVEILING OF WITNEY WAR MEMORIAL on 12 September 1920. All of the religious organizations in the town were present.

The Market Place, Witney. 910.

A GROUP OF CHILDREN POSE FOR THE PHOTOGRAPHER on the road between the Buttercross and the Town Hall in front of Corn Street. This would not be at all possible today.

"SUNLIGHT AND SHADOW," WITNEY TOWN HALL.

CORN STREET FROM THE TOWN HALL PIAZZA. You can just see the Red Lion public house (No. 1 Corn Street) in the centre at the bottom of Corn Street.

A POSTCARD VIEW OF CORN STREET dated 4 February 1934. It reads 'Having grand time here but a bit on the cold side but the air is pure more news later.'

MR AND MRS HOLLENS AND THEIR CHILDREN, Freda and Percy. Mr Hollens was manager of the Witney Steam Laundry in Corn Street. The family lived in Crofts House, The Crofts, and left Witney in September 1913.

THIS VIEW IS TAKEN MIDWAY UP CORN STREET, and beyond the laundry. The van on the left of the road, which offers removals to all parts, belongs to R.A. Jones. This firm still trades in Witney today.

CORN STREET, showing on the immediate right the premises of the Witney Laundry and Dry Cleaning Works Ltd.

CORN STREET, c. 1912.

LOWER CORN STREET, showing the premises of A.T. Horne, corn, cake, seed and manure merchant (Nos 156–60 Corn Street). This has now been replaced by M.A. Wilkin's showroom and antique shop.

CORN STREET, showing on the immediate right the Chequers Inn and beyond that Williams Brothers, timber and builders' merchants (No. 45 Corn Street and also at The Crofts).

CORN STREET, showing on the immediate right the premises of R.A. Jones (No. 45 Corn Street). The business was established in 1840, specializing in cabinet-making, upholstery and house clearance. They traded earlier from premises on the other side of the road.

THE GREAT WESTERN RAILWAY STATION at Witney at the beginning of the twentieth century. The station, which was on the Oxford to Fairford section, remained open until 1962 but there is little evidence of it left today.

Witney: the Southern End

WITNEY STATION. This branch of the Great Western system from Oxford to Witney was completed and opened for passenger traffic on 13 November 1861.

WITNEY STATION. The extension of the line to Fairford was opened in January 1874. The photograph is a postcard and is dated 1915. It was sent by Private C. Peskett (114406) of the Army Service Corps Motor Transport 347 Company, which was stationed at Witney.

PASSENGERS ALIGHTING FROM THE TRAIN at Witney station in 1908. The photograph was taken by Brice and Son of High Street, Witney.

THE 1ST WITNEY COMPANY BOYS' BRIGADE assembled at the station, c. 1906.

The Church from Railway Bridge, Witney.

THE LEYS AND ST MARY'S CHURCH from the railway bridge.

— THE LEYS. WITNEY OXON — 15 —

THE LEYS, sometimes known as Church Leys, was purchased in 1920 as a public recreation ground out of funds subscribed by Witney people, in memory of those who lost their lives in the First World War.

THE LEYS RECREATION GROUND. The photograph comes from a postcard sent on 12 August 1932, during a heatwave. It reads 'We have nearly melted away here in Witney.'

ON THE LEYS. This photograph is also a postcard and was produced by Frank Packer of Chipping Norton. It was sent on 20 August 1932. It reads 'Arrived safe and sound. Glorious weather, going to a Cricket match today.'

ANOTHER VIEW OF THE LEYS. The elegantly landscaped park was purchased for the town as part of the war memorial. Even in the early days it offered tennis courts, a bowling green, and a putting green as well as cricket, hockey and football pitches.

St. Mary's Church & Walk, Witney.

CHURCH WALK. The path connects Church Green and the Leys.

THE LEYS, looking towards Church Green and the Mount.

THE MOUNT HOUSE GATEWAY decorated for King George VI's coronation, 12 May 1937. The Land Army used the house as a hostel during the Second World War.

Witney Feast Fair

A GENERAL VIEW OF THE WITNEY FEAST, taken from the church tower, c. 1906.

WITNEY FEAST on 11 September 1905.

CROWDS AT THE FAIR, which was normally held on the Thursday following the first Sunday after 8 September.

TAYLOR'S ELECTRIC COLISEUM, entrance 3d., at the Witney Feast, c. 1906.

THE ELECTRIC LIVING PICTURE, another of Taylor's entertainments. The advertisement claimed that the show was 'bang up to date'.

AN EARLY PICTURE OF WITNEY FEAST in front of the church on Church Green. In later years the fair moved to the recreation ground, the Leys, behind the church.

THIS MERRY-GO-ROUND AT WITNEY MOP FAIR belonged to William Wilson and was known as the Rodeo Switchback. The photograph is dated 6 October 1926.

WITNEY FAIR, 1924. Rides included Studt's Chairs on the left, Wilson's Rodeo Switchback centre, Thurston's Steam Motors on the right, Nichol's Chairs and Gallopers, also on the right. There are also several other sets of steam rides evident.

SECTION FIVE

Witney at War

A PATRIOTIC PHOTOGRAPH encouraging residents of Witney to 'do their duty!'

SOLDIERS AND VEHICLES of the Army Service Corps Motor Transport 345 Company on Church Green.

GROUP PHOTOGRAPH OF SOLDIERS from 347 Company of the Motor Transport Army Service Corps in Witney prior to being posted abroad.

SOLDIERS OF 347 COMPANY on parade and ready for inspection. Believed to be on Church Green.

NO. 4 SECTION OF 347 COMPANY – a more formal photograph.

THE COMPANY BEING INSPECTED on Church Green in 1915.

SOLDIERS FROM 347 COMPANY NO. 8 SECTION relax by their vehicles.

TROOPS ASSEMBLED IN FRONT OF VEHICLES on the Leys, during the First World War.

CHILDREN, FAMILY AND FRIENDS join the soldiers from 347 Company for their sports day.

347 COMPANY SPORTS AT WITNEY. The picture is a postcard which reads 'I had a day flying yesterday. We had fifteen machines flying over here.' The date was 14 September 1915.

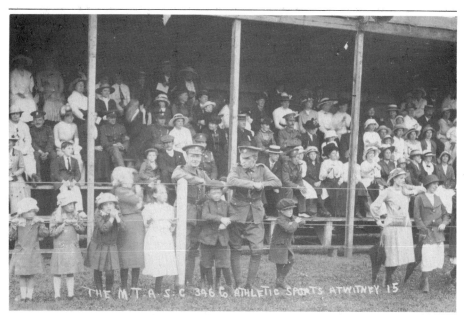

SOLDIERS AND SPECTATORS at the sports day.

CLOSE-UP OF SOLDIERS, VEHICLES AND EQUIPMENT at their Witney camp. This is a corner of the workshop section: note the anvil, bellows and forge.

Witney at Play

WITNEY GRAMMAR SCHOOL pupils and teachers around the maypole on the Leys. The photograph is a postcard dated 19 September 1905.

THE WITNEY BRITISH LEGION CARNIVAL, 1930. Of special interest is the decorated tricycle which is believed to pre-date the turn of the century.

THE BRITISH LEGION CARNIVAL, this time two years earlier.

THE FOOTBALLERS OF GORDON'S FOOTBALL CLUB in the 1906/7 season, from a photograph taken by Adams of Witney. The linesmen are seated at each end of the front row.

ANOTHER SPORTING PHOTOGRAPH, this time of the Witney Juniors football team in the 1906/7 season. Again this photograph was taken by Adams.

BEFORE THE MATCH. Chipping Norton versus Witney Workers' Union at Witney in 1914. Note the hayrick in the background and the size of the goal-mouth.

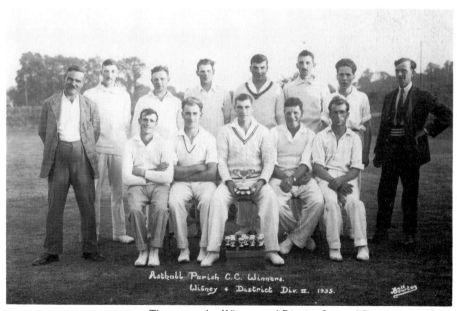

ASTHALL PARISH CRICKET TEAM. They won the Witney and District Second Division in 1935.

COMPANY SECTION BAND OF THE BOYS' BRIGADE at the Silver Jubilee celebrations in 1936, outside Rowley's shop.

BOY IN BOYS' BRIGADE UNIFORM (then known as the Lads' Brigade) on horseback, c. 1906.

Events in Witney

MILL WORKERS PREPARE FOR THE CARNIVAL. The building is believed to be the Newland Mill warehouse.

PROCESSION IN BRIDGE STREET of children, parents and teachers from the Wesleyan church and St Mary's Church of England school.

BRIDGE STREET MILL WORKERS assembled on the bridge. They are thought to be on strike.

A CLOSE-UP PHOTOGRAPH OF CHILDREN AND PARENTS assembling for the church treat, September 1906.

A PARTY CELEBRATING King George VI's coronation on 12 May 1937.

CHILDREN ASSEMBLE ON CHURCH GREEN to celebrate King George V's Silver Jubilee in 1935.

MRS JARLEY'S WAXWORKS. This was enacted by the teachers and others at the Wesleyan Bazaar in November 1904.

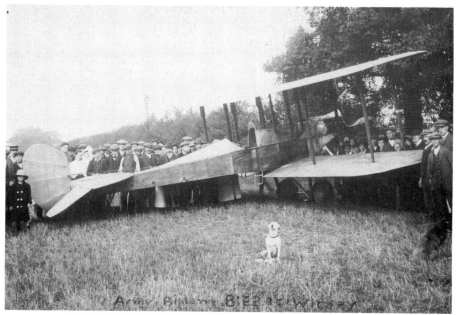

THIS MILITARY AIRCRAFT, a B.E. 2a, crash-landed on the Curbridge side of Witney in 1913.

EARLY'S BUILDING IN MILL STREET. The postcard reads 'This is the only one of the fire I can get, hope you will like it for your collection.'

The Woollen Industry

JAMES VANNER EARLY, mill owner, in his garden at Springfield House.

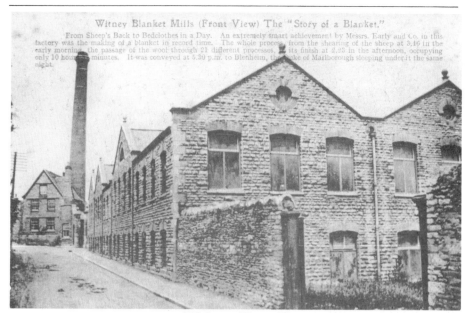

Witney Blanket Mills (Front View) The "Story of a Blanket."

From Sheep's Back to Bedclothes in a Day. An extremely smart achievement by Messrs. Early and Co. in this factory was the making of a blanket in record time. The whole process, from the shearing of the sheep at 3.40 in the early morning, the passage of the wool through 21 different processes, to its finish at 2.25 in the afternoon, occupying only 10 hours 45 minutes. It was conveyed at 3.30 p.m. to Blenheim, the Duke of Marlborough sleeping under it the same night.

THE EARLY AND CO. BLANKET MILL on Mill Street, Witney. The caption proudly documents the making of a blanket in record time for the Duke of Marlborough.

Early's Blanket Mills, Witney.

A REAR VIEW OF EARLY'S MILL, C. 1930. Later years saw extensive development as the business expanded.

ANOTHER VIEW OF EARLY'S MILL, C. 1940. The site looks much the same today.

Tentering and Drying Grounds, Mount Mills, Witney.

TENTERING AND DRYING GROUND, Mount Mill, off Church Green. The photograph was taken by Tomkins and Barrett of Swindon.

ONE DAY'S DELIVERY OF BLANKETS. This photograph was used by Charles Early and Co. for advertising.

The " Story of a Blanket," From Sheep's Back to Bedclothes in a Day. An extremely smart achievement by Messrs. Early & Co., in this factory, was the making of a blanket in record time. The whole process, from the shearing of the sheep at 3.46 in the early morning, the passage of the wool through 21 different processes, to its finish at 2.23 in the afternoon, occupying only 10 hours 37 minutes. It was conveyed at 5.30 p.m. to Blenheim, the Duke of Marlborough sleeping under it the same night.

THE WEAVING ROOM, Witney Blanket Mills, c. 1900. Many workers lost their hearing as a result of the noise the machines made.

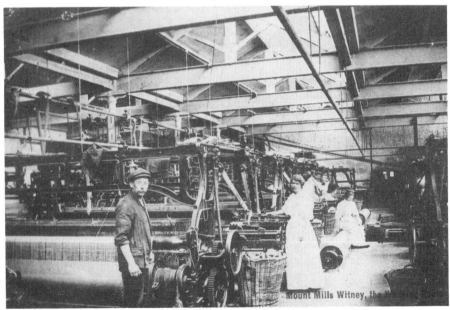

THE WEAVING ROOM – this time at Mount Mills, c. 1900. This is where the bobbins used for binding the edges of blankets were prepared.

THE CARDING AND SPINNING ROOM. The self-acting spinning mule is clearly visible.

MILL WORKERS, but more up to date. The photographer was Muriel Hewlett, but the names of the workers remain unknown.

THE ENTRANCE GATES TO THE WORKHOUSE, Tower Hill. In later years the building became the Crawford and Collet's works.

THE NEW PREMISES OF THE WITNEY BLANKET CO. LTD on the Leys. This is now a superstore.

A PICTURE OF THE BUTTERCROSS used by the blanket company for advertising. Witney's heritage, it implies, is intertwined with the tradition of blanket manufacture. On the reverse side it reads: 'Under the severe test of constant use, and in the interest of hygiene there are blankets in every home that require cleaning . . . from time to time you will have to renew the life and usefulness of your blankets by sending them to be refinished.'

WITNEY MILL AFTER THE BLAZE, 1905. This scene of the aftermath comes from a postcard, which reads 'I think you can remember the night this happened and how the Oxford Brigade came rushing up. The damage was estimated at £7,000 and was caused by a bearing getting hot.'

THE FIRE AT WITNEY MILL occurred on Wednesday 11 January 1905 and lasted well into the night, as shown in the picture below.

THE MILL ABLAZE, 11 January 1905. The photograph was produced as a postcard, which was on sale the day after the fire.

A pair of Merino Wool Blankets, with his monogram worked in Silk, was made in this Factory and sent as a birthday present to the Right Hon. William Ewart Gladstone in his eighty-third year. The cost of the material (£5), was subscribed by the employees, Messrs. W. Smith and Co. providing the labour.

BRIDGE STREET MILLS, which was extensively damaged by fire in July 1990. It had not been used as a mill for many years but housed several small business units.

SECTION NINE

Oddments

WITNEY FIRE BRIGADE in the 1920s. The cap badges read WFB (Witney Fire Brigade). The pump is steam-powered.

THIS SUPER-SENTINEL THREE-WAY TIPPER LORRY was powered by steam, had solid, pneumatic tyres, and was built in 1925 for the Witney Transport Company. The maximum speed permitted was 12 m.p.h., reduced to 5 m.p.h. when a trailer was attached.

AN ACCIDENT TO BUTTERCROSS, C. 1904. The Buttercross was built in 1683 by William Blake of Cogges, and renovated in 1811 and 1868. It is a wooden structure, supported by thirteen cylindrical pillars; it has four gables at the cardinal points, and at the apex of the roof is a square turret with an illuminated clock; the basement was used at one time on market days for the sale of butter, poultry, eggs and other commodities.

A WEDDING SNAPSHOT. The groom was Frederick Oswald Whitcher (his shop is featured on p. 46), the bride Miss Ada Annie Trevarthen from Cornwall. The marriage took place one Tuesday at the Wesleyan chapel, Witney. The newspaper reports 'During the evening the happy couple drove to Oxford en route for Devoran, Cornwall, where the honeymoon is to be spent. They were the recipients of numerous useful presents.'

THE WOMEN'S LAND ARMY. The organization used the Mount as a hostel in the Second World War.

A POSTCARD VIEW OF THE TANK ON TOWER HILL after it had burst. The event caused some amusement, as the poem on the back suggests.

"HINC ILLÆ LACHRYMÆ."

Rejected, scorned,
    Poor old Tank ;
Piece by piece to earth
    It sank !   R.I.P.

Old girders gone—
    The new arrive ;
A better job to make
    They strive.

A nice YOUNG Tank
    Grows up each day,
Until at last it seems
    To say—

"Oh, fill me up with
    Water more," (Moore)
And in the stream begins
    To pour.

Proudly it gleams with
    Colour bright ;
Its bright red paint
    Dazzles sight.

Pride goes before a fall
    They say,
And so it seemed to be
    That day !

For all at once the side
    Fell out !
Contents poured out like a
    Water spout !

What fate is this that seems
    To hang
About this Tower, makes Tanks
    Go bang ?

Is it to keep those names
    On view ?
Or keep their owners in
    A stew ?

Oh, poor old Tank ! poor
    YOUNG one too !
Alas, that we should mourn
    For you !

THESE PICTURES SHOW THE TOWN CREST, with the influence of the wool trade clearly evident. In the scroll is the town's motto 'Weave truth with trust'.

QRA :

**17, CORN STREET,
WITNEY,
OXON,
ENGLAND**

●

R.S.G.B.

G3HG

ADIO G3YH   Sigs   T   RST 589

                                              QSB to R   nil

KD ERE APRIL   AT 900   GMT   QRG 7.7 MC.

MNI TKS FER CARD ES QSO, S UP HPE U AGN SN.

CVR 8 VALVE SUPER   MIT L6 CO & 6L7 PA.

SE QSL TNX OM.   ER   T OF LE FLEX

RECT or via R.S.G.B.   INPUT   10 WATTS

                    VY 73's   VICTOR DELNEVO.

Print by G6DS

A QSL CARD sent by Victor Delnevo of No. 17 Corn Street, Witney, to another amateur broadcaster in Hall Street, Bristol, in confirmation of a radio contact made on short wave on 18 June 1946.

THE ALMSHOUSES, WITNEY. These were founded by John Holloway for six weavers' widows. The same number were erected by William Townshend at the bottom of Oxford Road, near Broad Hill, and were for single women, with an allowance of 4s. 6d. per week.

The Villages around Witney

Aston Church

THE PARISH CHURCH AT ASTON, two miles east of Bampton and four-and-a-half miles south of Witney. The church of St James, erected in 1839, was restored between 1885–9 at a cost of £563.

THE TOWN HALL, BAMPTON, five miles south-west of Witney. The building was erected in 1840 and extended in 1906. The upper rooms were used for public meetings and the ground-floor room housed the fire engine. In the background is J. Eeles, grocery.

THE MANOR HOUSE, BAMPTON. The photograph was produced by 'Martin, printer and stationer of the Post Office, Bampton' c. 1906.

AN UNUSUAL VIEW OF LEW, three-and-a-half miles south-west of Witney. The principal landowner for many years was Christ Church, Oxford.

ST BARTHOLOMEW'S CHURCH AND SCHOOL, Ducklington, two miles south-west of Witney. The church, built in a mixture of styles, was renovated and restored in 1872 and then again ten years later. The parochial school catered for both boys and girls. In 1869 the mistress was Miss Emeline Toombs.

The Fish-House
Cokethorpe

THE FISH-HOUSE, COKETHORPE, about one mile south-east of Ducklington. Opposite the fish-house is Cokethorpe Park, containing a fine mansion built in 1711, which for some time was the home of the poet John Gay. The building is now used as a school.

THE GOLDEN BALLS, STANDLAKE, about five miles south-east of Witney. The photograph is of Charles W. Siret's 'beanfeast', the annual dinner given to his employees.

A VIEW OF THE VILLAGE, NORTHMOOR, seven miles south-east of Witney. The church of St Denys dates from the period between the Early English and Decorated styles, and the interior was restored and re-opened on 12 April 1887.

THE DOVE-COT, NORTHMOOR, c. 1920.

THE ROSE REVIVED PUBLIC HOUSE, NEWBRIDGE, seven miles south-east of Witney. The photograph was taken in the 1930s and the place is much the same today.

THE MAYBUSH INN, NEWBRIDGE. This is an early photograph of the inn, which stands on the opposite side of the river to the Rose Revived. Note the boats and the people relaxing in the inn's garden.

THE FERRY AT BABLOCK HYTHE, six-and-a-half miles south-east of Witney. The photograph shows the ferry that crossed the Thames to provide an easy route to Cumnor. Evidence of the ferry winch remains today.

A VIEW OF STANTON HARCOURT, five miles south-east of Witney. Many of the cottages shown in the photograph remain much the same today.

The Church, Stanton Harcourt.

THE CHURCH, STANTON HARCOURT, viewed from the Manor grounds. Parts of the church (St Michael's) date back to the twelfth century. The other building is known as Pope's Tower. Alexander Pope, the poet, stayed at the Manor House between 1716 – 18 and is said to have finished the fifth volume of his translation of Homer's *Iliad* when there.

THE HARCOURT ARMS, STANTON HARCOURT, c. 1895. The premises have been significantly altered and extended in recent years.

The Stocks, Stanton Harcourt.

THE STOCKS, STANTON HARCOURT. The village stocks are still standing today, a short distance from the Manor House. In 1939 Viscount Harcourt was lord of the manor, the house having been held by the family for more than seven hundred and fifty years.

Crawley Blanket Mills, Witney

THE SMITH'S BLANKET MILLS, Crawley, two miles north of Witney. The mill is situated in a hollow about one mile west of Hailey. The other major building is St Peter's church, built in 1837 at a cost of £250.

THE CHURCH AND RUINS, Minster Lovell, two-and-three-quarter miles north-west of Witney. St Kenelm church and the ancient mansion (now in ruins) were built by Lord William Lovel between 1425 and 1465.

Minster Lovell

THE VILLAGE OF MINSTER LOVELL, C. 1920. Close to the village is Charterville, which was an allotment estate containing eighty small farms of 2, 3 and 4 acres, each with a one-floor cottage. The estate was laid out in 1847 as part of Feargus O'Connor's land scheme. Some of the cottages can still be seen today.

THE WESLEYAN CHURCH, HAILEY, two miles north of Witney. The church was built in 1908. Later it was sold and has now been converted into a private residence.

ST JOHN THE EVANGELIST CHURCH, HAILEY. The old church was virtually demolished in 1868 and the materials were used to erect a new church, built in 1868/9 at a cost of £200 on a new site given by the Revd George Crabb Rolfe, vicar of the parish between 1858–93.

ST JAMES' CHURCH, RAMSDEN, four miles north of Witney. The church was erected in 1872. The other important buildings in the village were the school, Methodist chapel and Ramsden House.

THE POST OFFICE, SOUTH LEIGH, two-and-a-half miles south-east of Witney. The village retains much of its charm today. Of special interest is the old manor house near the church.

THE VILLAGE, NORTH LEIGH, four miles north-east of Witney. The village landmark is the windmill which regrettably stands derelict today. Much of the character of the village has changed as a result of recent developments.

THE GREEN, COMBE, six miles north-east of Witney. The original site of the village and church is said to have been in the adjoining valley of Evenlode: the mounds by the mill probably mark the ancient church.